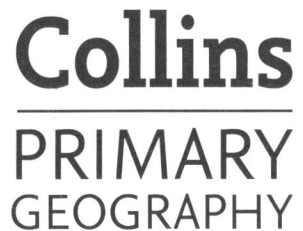

Collins PRIMARY GEOGRAPHY

Movement
Workbook 4

Planet Earth

Coasts
The seashore — 2
Shaping the coast — 4
Exploring the coast — 6

Water

Rivers
Describing rivers — 8
Rivers matter — 10
Managing rivers — 12

Weather

Weather patterns
Extreme weather — 14
Weather forecasts — 16
Recording the weather — 18

Settlements

Towns
Understanding towns — 20
The origin of towns — 22
Town life — 24

Work and Travel

Food and shops
Farms and food — 26
From farm to supermarket — 28
Local shops — 30

Environment

Caring for towns
Old and new buildings — 32
Making improvements — 34
Comparing places — 36

Places

Northern Ireland — 38
Germany — 44
North America — 50
Asia — 56

Fiona Macgregor

Unit 1 Coasts

Lesson 1: The seashore

1 a) Draw lines to match the captions to the photographs.

sandy beach, Portrush

rocky coastline, Cornwall

mudflats, Essex

shingle bank, Highlands

b) Where are these places in the UK? Look at the map on page 2 of your Pupil Book. Write the correct numbers from the map in the small boxes.

Unit 1 **Coasts**

2 a) Draw a picture map of an imaginary island. Show three or more different coastlines on your map.

b) Label the different types of coastline on your map. Use the words in the boxes to help you.

(sandy beach) (mudflat) (shingle bank) (rocky coastline) (cliffs)

c) Make up names for each of your coastlines.

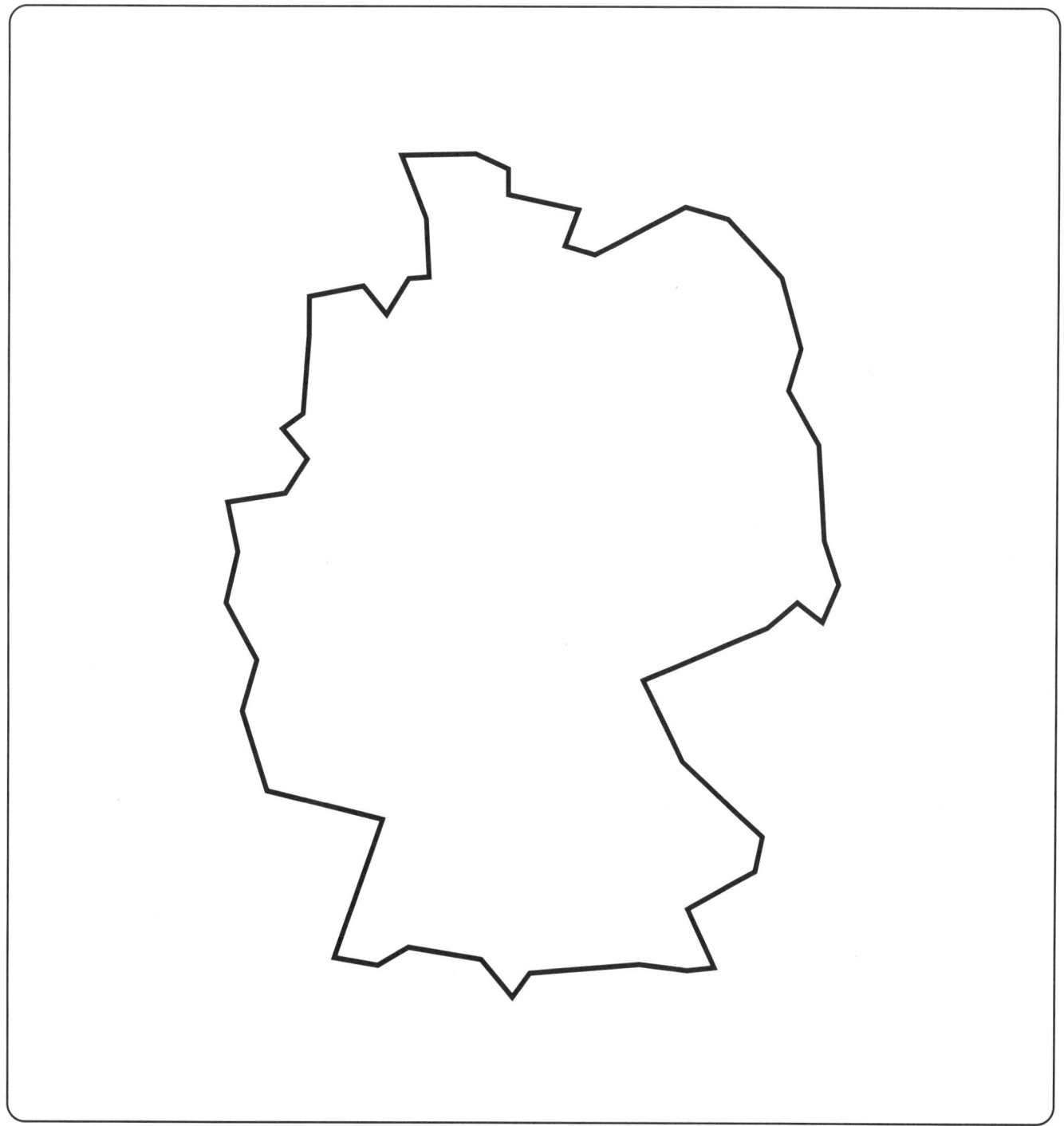

➜ Supports Pupil Book Mapwork, page 3

Unit 1 Coasts

Lesson 2: Shaping the coast

❶ Look at the image of a coastline.

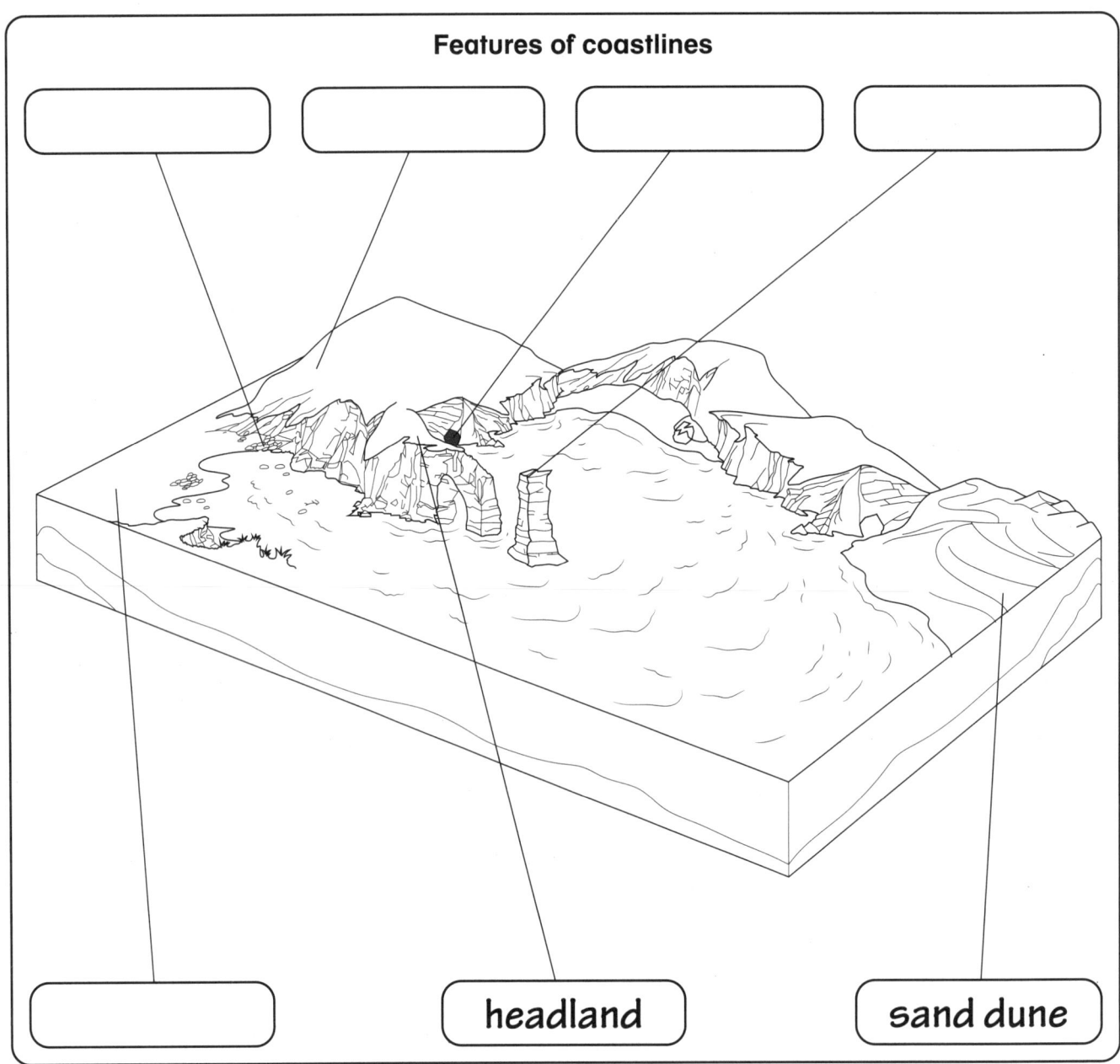

a) Colour the key.

b) Colour the drawing using the colours you chose.

c) Add the labels below to the drawing in the correct places.

headland | beach | sand dune | cliff
boulders | cave | rock stack

Key

cliffs	
sea	
sand	
grass	

➔ Supports Pupil Book Investigation, page 5

Unit 1 Coasts

❷ Study the two drawings.

  a) Circle all the differences.

  b) Write a sentence explaining each of the differences you found.

  The sandy beach has grown larger.

  The headland has

  A cave

  Sand dunes

5

Unit 1 Coasts

Lesson 3: Exploring the coast

1 a) Draw lines to match the names to the pictures.

| barnacles | flowers | worm | jellyfish |

b) Where are these plants and creatures found on the seashore? Use the words from the boxes above to label the picture.

Hint: Look at Pupil Book page 7 if you need help.

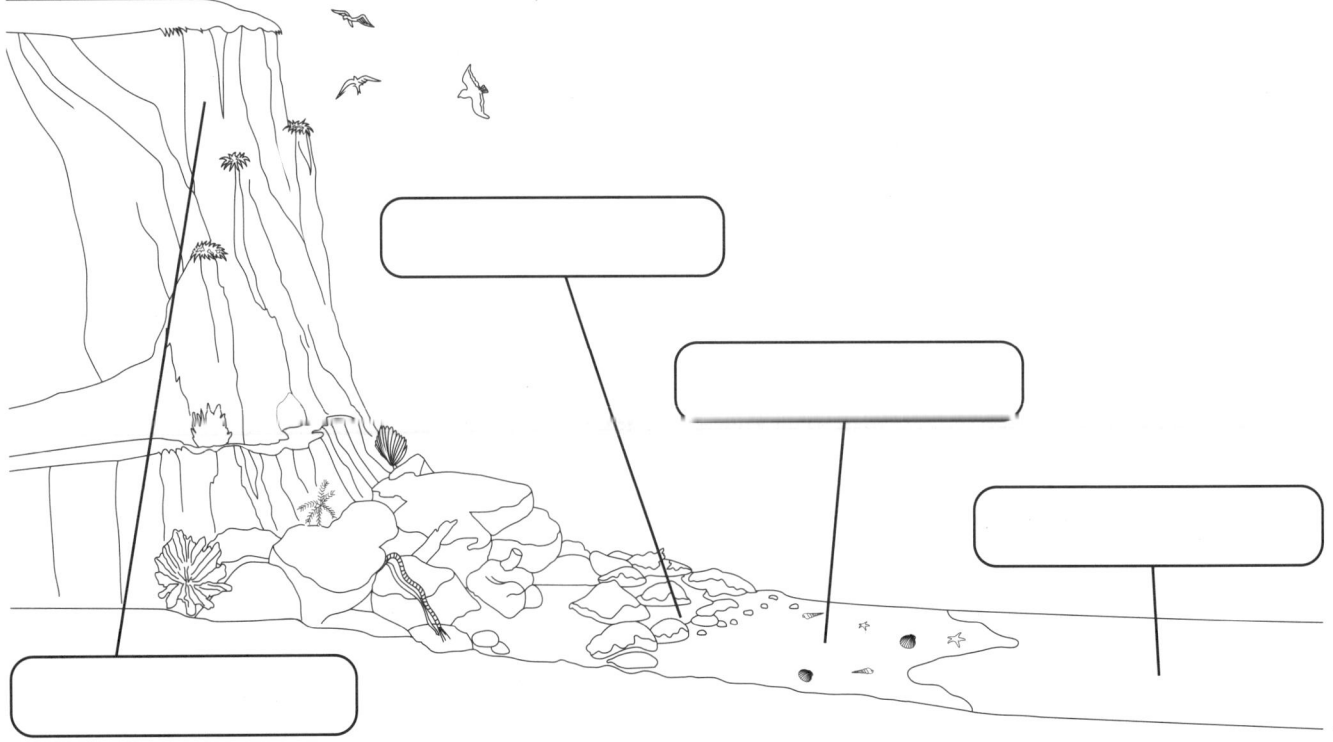

Unit 1 Coasts

❷ Find these words about Sidmouth in the wordsearch puzzle.

groynes · garden · litter bins · ladder · boulders · cliff
pier · beach · concrete wall · Chit Rocks · River Sid · town

g	r	o	y	n	e	s	u	q	p	n	l
a	q	p	z	v	w	c	r	h	i	d	i
r	v	a	i	c	l	i	f	f	e	y	t
d	p	l	b	r	o	d	m	p	r	q	t
e	r	i	v	e	r	s	i	d	y	c	e
n	h	q	k	j	g	h	w	j	m	l	r
w	b	o	u	l	d	e	r	s	t	r	b
g	e	x	s	z	y	s	t	o	w	n	i
o	a	u	f	e	n	l	i	b	k	x	n
a	c	m	c	h	i	t	r	o	c	k	s
e	h	f	z	t	w	l	a	d	d	e	r
c	o	n	c	r	e	t	e	w	a	l	l

❸ Write three sentences about what you have found out about the coastline. Draw small pictures in the boxes to represent your three findings.

_____
_____
_____

→ Supports Pupil Book Investigation, page 6

Unit 2 Rivers

Lesson 1: Describing rivers

1 a) Put the parts of the story 'The Salmon' in the correct order. Number the parts 1 to 6 in the boxes.

☐ The salmon swam on as the river started to **meander** across the flatter lands.

☐ One day it swam out of the pool and into the **stream**.

☐ The salmon reached the **estuary** which fed into the sea.

☐ The stream turned into a river, where the water moved really quickly.

☐ The salmon was born in a **pool** high up in the hills.

☐ The river water became deeper and started to taste salty.

b) Draw lines to match the key words to their definitions.

| meander | where a river joins the sea |

| stream | bend and curve |

| estuary | a small river |

| pool | a deep, slow-moving area of water |

8

Unit 2   Rivers

2 Make up a poem or write a sentence about a river. Arrange the words so they meander across the page like a flowing river. Look at the example sentence first.

Rivers begin as tiny streams in hills and mountains.

→ Supports Pupil Book Investigation, page 8

Unit 2 Rivers

Lesson 2: Rivers matter

1 Imagine you are taking a journey from Lake Victoria to Cairo, along the River Nile.

a) Trace your route on the map.

b) Make a list of all the places you would pass on your route.

_____
_____
_____
_____
_____
_____
_____
_____
_____
_____

Murchison Falls is also known as Kabalega Falls.

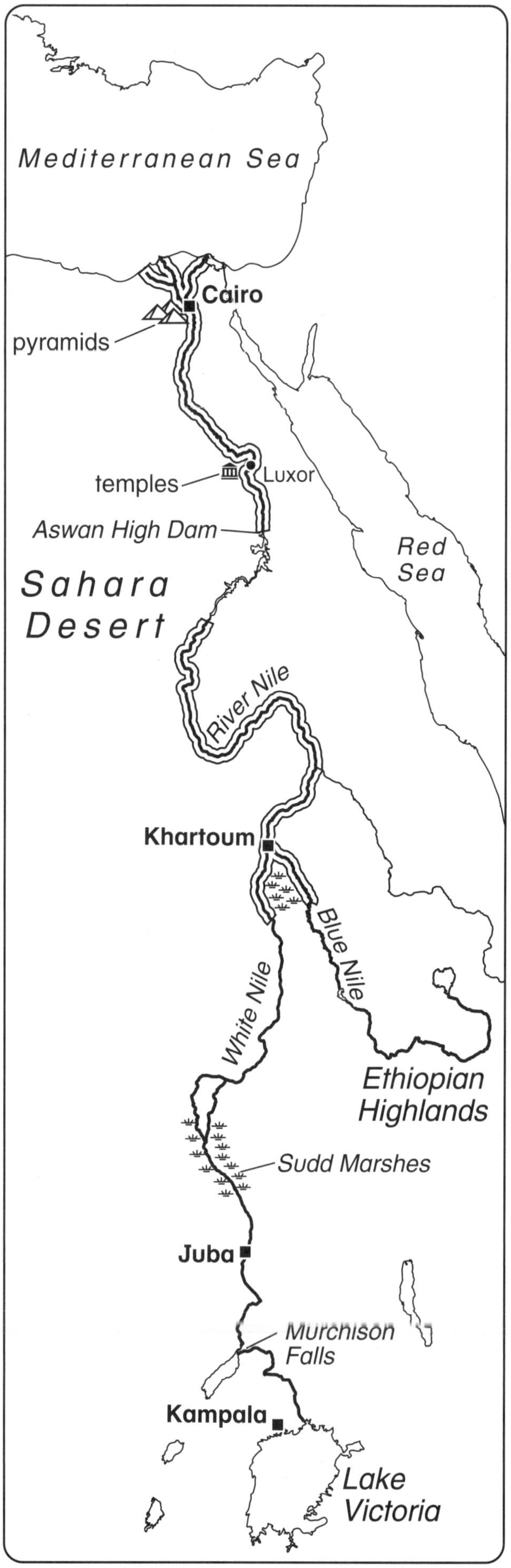

Unit 2   Rivers

2 a) Use pages 10 and 11 of your Pupil Book to write five interesting questions about the River Nile. Leave space for the answers.

Question 1: _____
_____
Answer: _____
_____

Question 2: _____
_____
Answer: _____
_____

Question 3: _____
_____
Answer: _____
_____

Question 4: _____
_____
Answer: _____
_____

Question 5: _____
_____
Answer: _____
_____

b) Swap your book with a friend and answer each other's questions.

Unit 2 Rivers

Lesson 3: Managing rivers

❶ Describe what is happening in each of these pictures.
Write captions to say what is happening, and why.

Unit 2 Rivers

❷ Read the information about the Sumida River, Tokyo on page 13 of your Pupil Book.

Write three facts about the Sumida River in the top three boxes in the diagram.

❸ Research two more facts about the Sumida River. Write them in the bottom boxes.

Hint: You could research these facts:
- What birds and animals live on the river?
- What different types of boat use the river?

Unit 3 Weather patterns

Lesson 1: Extreme weather

1 a) Choose the best words from the word bank to go with each picture. Write the words in the space provided. Use each word once.

b) Colour in each picture. Use colours and shading to emphasise the extreme weather.

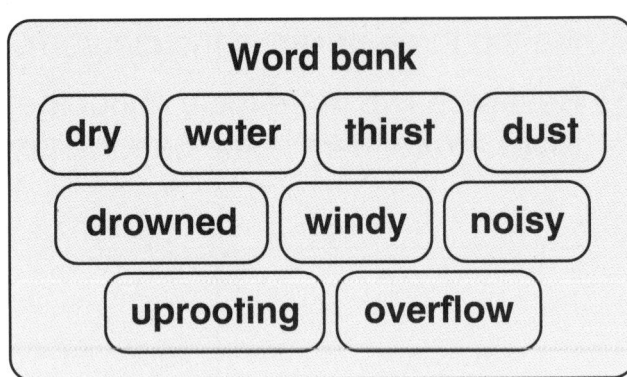

Word bank

dry   water   thirst   dust
drowned   windy   noisy
uprooting   overflow

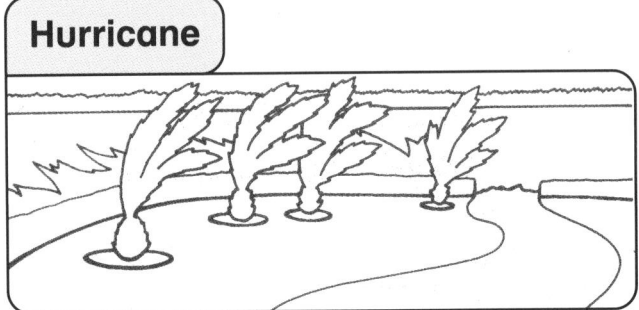

Hurricane

Best words _____ _____

Flood

Best words _____ _____

Drought

Best words _____ _____

2 What kind of weather do you think does the most damage? Give reasons for your answer.

_____

_____

_____

14

Unit 3 Weather patterns

3 a) Look at this picture. Label all the things you can see.

b) Now imagine there was a huge storm with high winds, heavy rain and flooding. Draw the damage you think could happen to the things in the picture.

Unit 3 Weather patterns

Lesson 2: Weather forecasts

1 Look at this weather forecast for the week and answer the questions.

Hint: This type of forecast shows the highest (hottest) temperature for the day at the top, and the lowest (coldest) temperature for the day below.

a) On which three days will there be at least some sunshine?

_____

b) Write the two days that have the same highest temperature.

_____   _____

c) Which day is going to have the coldest lowest temperature?

_____

d) If you were going out on Saturday, what would you wear?

_____

e) Which day has the biggest difference between the high temperature for that day and the low temperature for that day?

Hint: To find the difference, subtract the low temperature from the high temperature.

_____

Unit 3 Weather patterns

2 Study this weather map of Europe.

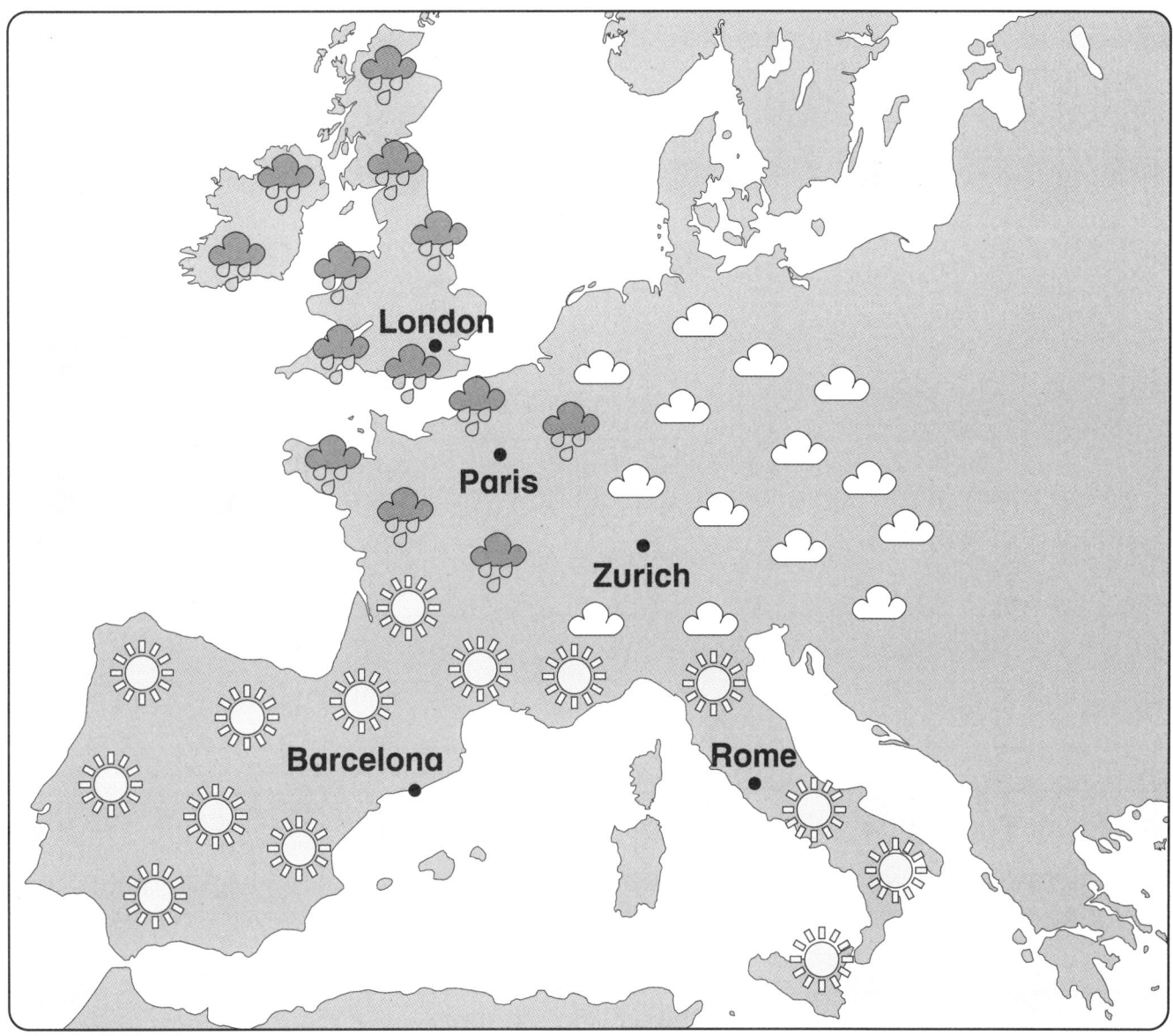

Write a simple weather report, saying what the weather is going to be like in the cities shown on the map.

Zurich: **In Zurich, Switzerland, it is going to be cloudy today.**

London: _____

Paris: _____

Barcelona: _____

Rome: _____

Hint: Use an atlas or the internet to find out the countries for each city.

Unit 3 Weather patterns

Lesson 3: Recording the weather

1 Look at the photograph and the drawing of an **anemometer**.

 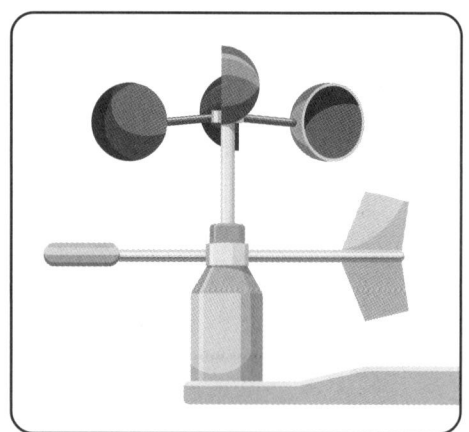

anemometer: a weather recording instrument that measures the speed of wind.

Write two or three sentences to explain how you think an anemometer measures wind.

_____

_____

_____

2 Look at the pictures of the wind on page 18 of your Pupil Book.

Hint: You could draw washing on a line or a tent being put up – use your imagination!

a) Draw your own pictures to show the force of the wind. Use a different example to the tree.

force 0	force 3	force 6	force 8

b) Use your wind scale in part **a)** to record the strength of the wind, where you live, for five days.

Monday	Tuesday	Wednesday	Thursday	Friday
_____	_____	_____	_____	_____

Unit 3   **Weather patterns**

3 a) Draw your own weather symbols, for example:

b) Use your symbols to record the weather at your school for two weeks. Complete the chart.

Day	Week 1	Week 2
Monday		
Tuesday		
Wednesday		
Thursday		
Friday		

c) Write a short report about the weather over the two weeks. Did it change throughout the weeks? Did it affect the things you did?

_____
_____
_____
_____
_____
_____

➜ Supports Pupil Book Investigation, page 19

Unit 4 Towns

Lesson 1: Understanding towns

❶ Look at the map and photograph of East Kilbride on page 21 of your Pupil Book. Where are these places? Write the grid references.

a) the Old Parish __B3__

b) the swimming pool (two grid squares) _____ _____

c) parkland _____

d) houses and flats (two options) _____ _____

e) the car park _____

❷ a) Draw a picture of one important building in your nearest town.

b) Write a sentence saying what type of building this is, and why it is important.

	Why I chose this building:
	_____
	_____
	_____
	_____
	_____
	_____
	_____
	_____
	_____
	_____
	_____
	_____

Unit 4 Towns

❸ Look at this town, viewed from above.

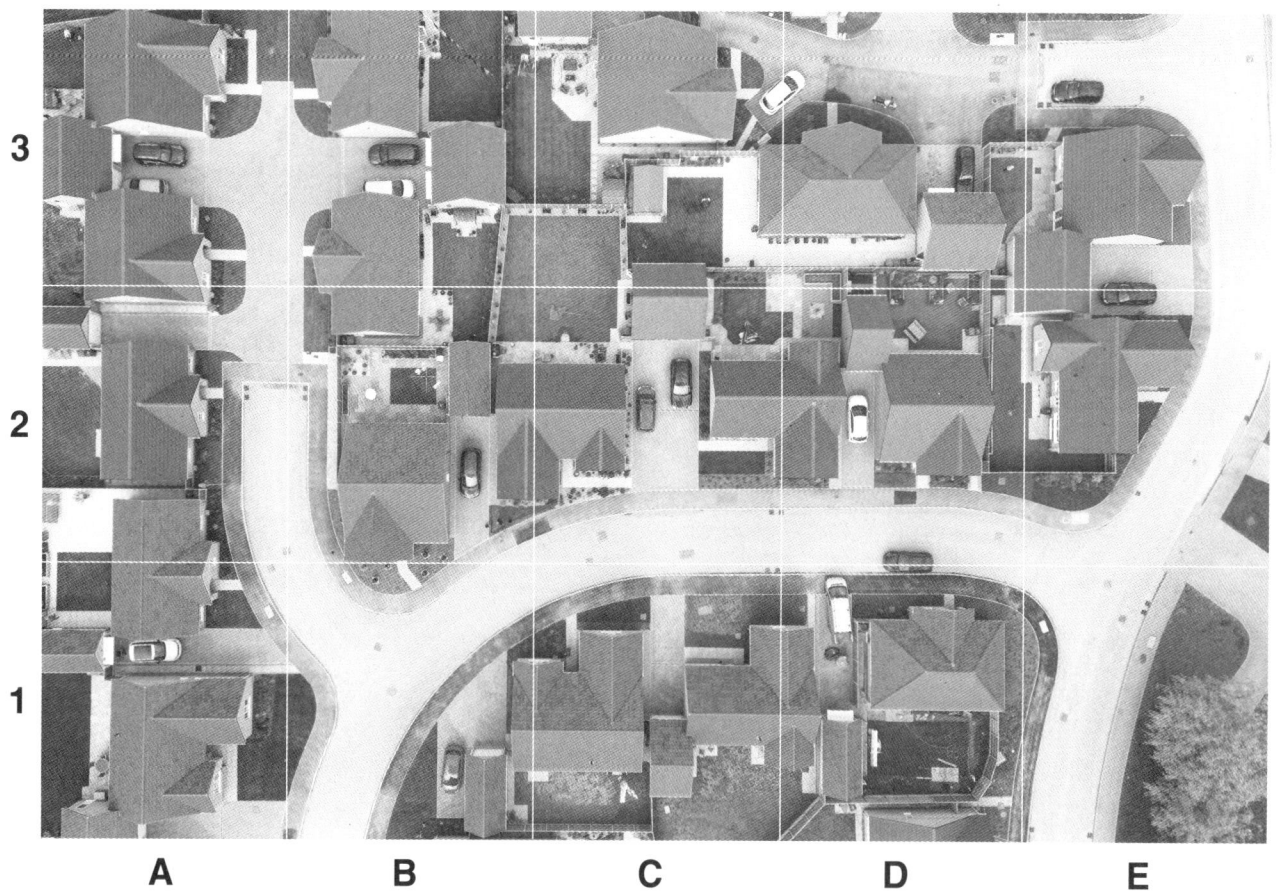

A   B   C   D   E

Now use the grid to draw a simple map of the area. Include the roads and houses.

A   B   C   D   E

Unit 4 Towns

Lesson 2: The origin of towns

1 What types of towns do these photographs show? Use the words in the boxes to write labels for each image.

- market town
- factory town
- seaside resort
- port

Guangzhou, China

Type of town:

_____

Wittenberg, Germany

Type of town:

_____

Lamu, Kenya

Type of town:

_____

Lyttelton, New Zealand

Type of town:

_____

Unit 4 Towns

2 a) Use a map or the internet to find out information about your nearest town.

The name of the town:	What kind of town did it start as?
What is it known for?	What are the names of some of the schools in the town?
Does it have factories? If yes, write the factory names.	Does it have a bridge or a port? If yes, write their names.
Where do people shop? Write the names of some of the shops or markets.	Is there an old part of town and a new part of town? Describe these areas.

b) Take a photograph of the town, or find a picture of the town, and stick it here.

Unit 4 Towns

Lesson 3: Town life

1 Look at the examples of some things children found in their nearest town. Choose four things you can find in your nearest town.

  a) Draw a picture of each thing or stick in a photo.

  b) Write a sentence to explain how each one helps to keep the town working.

This is a: _____

It helps the town because:

_____

_____

This is a: _____

It helps the town because:

_____

_____

This is a: _____

It helps the town because:

_____

_____

This is a: _____

It helps the town because:

_____

_____

→ Supports Pupil Book Investigation, page 25

Unit 4 Towns

❷ Plan your own town, and make a map of it. You can copy these building symbols, or you can draw your own symbols.

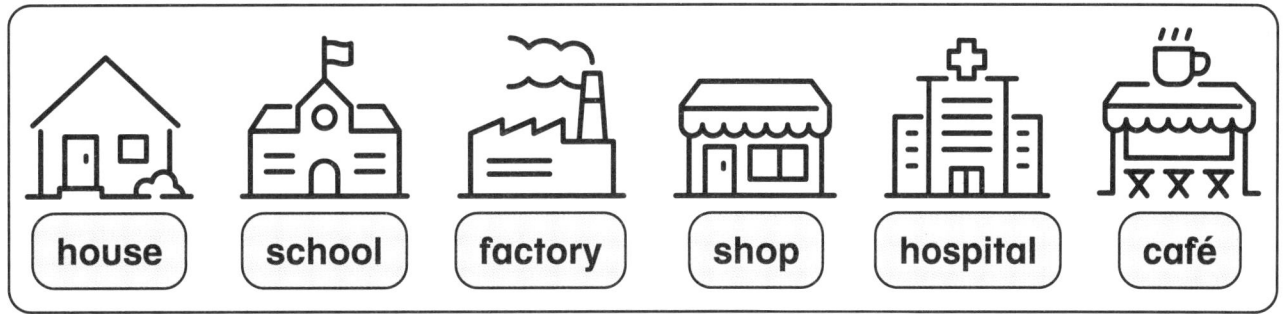

a) Start by deciding where your town is. Is it on a river? At the seaside? At a crossroads?

b) First draw the roads. Keep it simple.

c) Then decide where to place your buildings (for example, houses should be close to schools).

d) Give your town a name.

Unit 5   Food and shops

Lesson 1: Farms and food

1 Do some research to find out more information about dairy farms. Fill in the boxes with as much information as you can.

Overview

What is a dairy farm?

_____

_____

Weather

What type of weather is best for a dairy farm? Why?

_____

_____

_____

_____

Near me

Where is your nearest dairy farm?

_____

_____

Produce

What food and drinks are made from dairy? Write a list of as many items as you can.

_____

_____

_____

_____

_____

_____

Unit 5 Food and shops

❷ Look at the map on page 26 of your Pupil Book.

a) Use two colours to colour the key.

b) Colour the map to show the areas of the UK that are good for farmers growing crops, and the areas that are better for farmers keeping cows and sheep. Use the same colours as your key.

Key

crops	
cows and sheep	

❸ Find out about the kind of farming that happens near where you live.

a) Do farmers grow crops? What kind?

_____

_____

_____

_____

b) Do farmers keep animals? What kind?

_____

c) What sort of landscape is there near where you live?

_____

d) What sort of weather do you have?

_____

e) Find out what sort of soil you have. For example, wet and boggy, or dry and rocky, or something else.

_____

Unit 5 Food and shops

Lesson 2: From farm to supermarket

❶ Draw pictures in the empty circles to show how pineapples are imported from Sri Lanka.

❷ Add arrows to link the pictures in the correct order.

Growing

Packing

Selling

Transporting

Distributing

Unit 5 **Food and shops**

3 a) Imagine you are importing oranges from Turkey to the UK by lorry. Draw the route the oranges would take.

- **Think!** Will the route go across water? Use a different colour to show the route for ships.

b) What countries does your route pass through? Use a more detailed map or atlas to help you.

→ Supports Pupil Book Mapwork, page 29

Unit 5 Food and shops

Lesson 3: Local shops

❶ Which of these shops do you think you have in your nearest town? Circle the shops.

Type of shop					
Food	Clothes	Household	Furniture	Refreshments	Money/offices
baker butcher greengrocer mini market supermarket	charity clothes shoes sports	books chemist electrical florist newsagents toys	antiques carpets furniture	café fast food restaurant	bank estate agents post office travel
Others: hotel, hairdresser, music shop					

❷ a) Take a notebook with you when you next visit your nearest town. Write the names of as many shops as you can see, and what they sell.

b) Sort your list of shops into the groups shown in Activity 1 and write them in the table below. How many shops did you see from each group? Write the number at the bottom of each column.

Type of shop					
Food	Clothes	Household	Furniture	Refreshments	Money/offices
Others:					

→ Supports Pupil Book Investigation, page 30

Unit 5   **Food and shops**

3 a) Record your results in a bar graph.

- Colour one block for each shop.
- Use different colours for the different types of shops.
- Make a key to show which colour represents which type of shop.

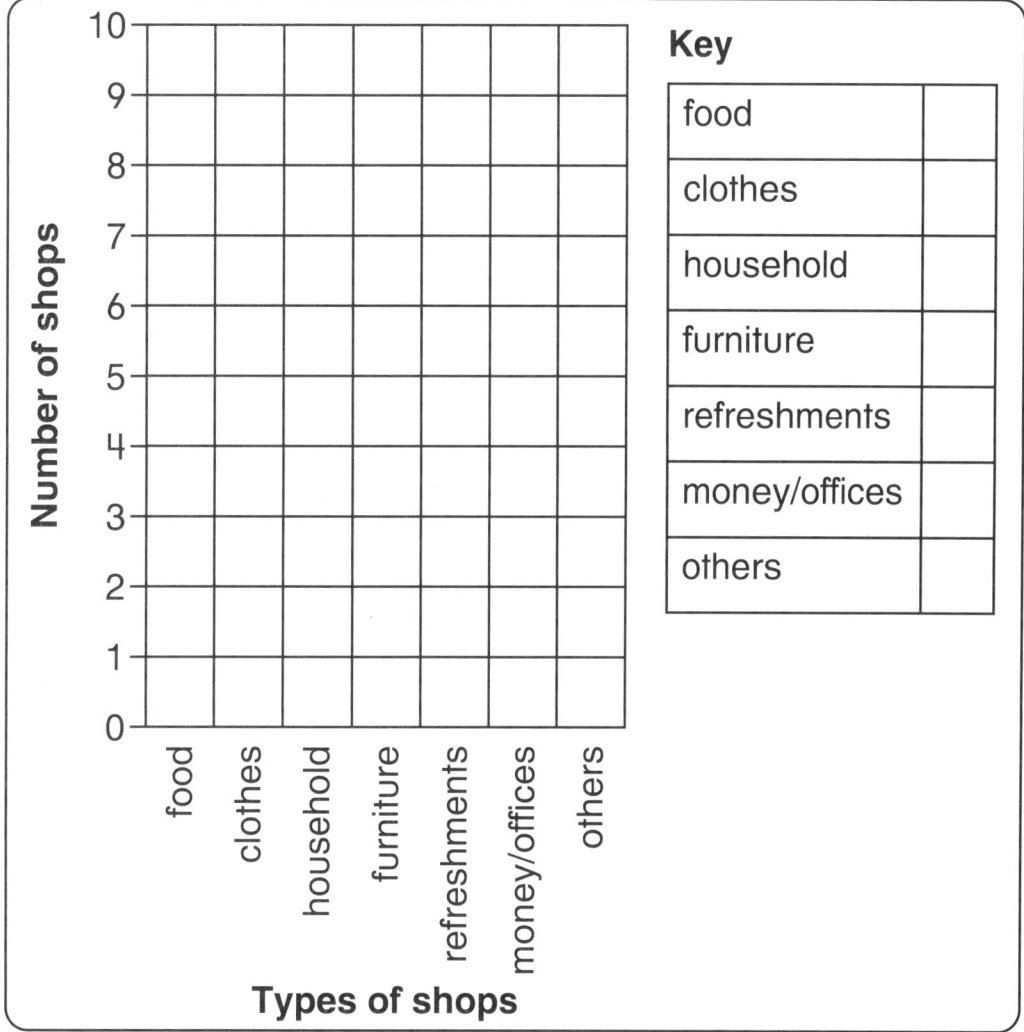

b) Write a short paragraph about what were the most common shops, and what were the least common shops.

_____
_____
_____
_____

→ Supports Pupil Book Investigation, page 30

Unit 6   Caring for towns

Lesson 1: Old and new buildings

1 a) Study the old windmill.

broken sail

cracks in the bricks

door hanging from its hinges

mill stone in the grass

b) Now draw a plan to show how you could convert this windmill into a house with three floors.

> **Hint:** Think about which rooms would go on which floor – living area, kitchen, bathrooms, bedrooms. How would you get from room to room?

c) Label each room in your plan.

➜ Supports Pupil Book Mapwork, page 33

Unit 6 — Caring for towns

2 a) Find out about a historic or protected building in your area.

b) Find a photograph of the building and stick it below, or do a drawing of the building in the space below.

c) Write a short paragraph about why you think this building is interesting. Remember to:
- give the name of the building
- say where it is
- give facts about its history or why it is protected
- say why you find it interesting.

_____

_____

_____

_____

➜ Supports Pupil Book Investigation, page 33

Unit 6 — Caring for towns

Lesson 2: Making improvements

1 a) Add to the drawing to improve this pedestrianised street. Use the ideas in the word boxes. You can add more of your own ideas, too.

attractive street lamps   paved shopping area

bollards   bins   places to sit

b) Draw lines to match the word boxes to where they are in your drawing.

Unit 6 **Caring for towns**

2 **a)** Look at this photograph of an area in a town.

> **Hint:** See Pupil Book page 35 for examples of improvement schemes.

How would you improve this area? Write your ideas.

_____
_____
_____
_____

b) Draw a sketch of the changes you would make.

35

Unit 6 | Caring for towns

Lesson 3: Comparing places

1 Look at the photographs of these two schools. Then answer the questions.

a) How do you think people travel to school?
_____
_____

b) What is the same about each school?
_____
_____

c) What is different about each school?
_____
_____

d) What street furniture would you add to the areas? Why?
_____
_____

Unit 6   **Caring for towns**

❷ Make a survey of your area.

    a) Think of four areas that you think could be improved.

    b) Draw a picture of the improvement you would make in each of the areas you have chosen.

    c) Write a caption explaining the change that you would make.

Unit 7 — Northern Ireland

Lesson 1: Introducing Northern Ireland

1 a) Choose two of these landscape features in Northern Ireland. Colour in your choices.

- River Bann
- Sperrin Mountains
- Lough Neagh
- Antrim Hills
- Mourne Mountains
- Giant's Causeway

b) Find a photograph or draw a picture of the two landscape features.

c) Find out an interesting fact about the two features. Write the fact next to the picture.

	Name of feature: _____ **Interesting fact:** _____ _____ _____ _____ _____
	Name of feature: _____ **Interesting fact:** _____ _____ _____ _____ _____

Unit 7 Northern Ireland

2 a) Read the table showing some of the ferry routes from Northern Ireland.

b) Draw the routes on the map. Use a different colour for each ferry route.

Ferry routes

Belfast Northern Ireland	⇄	Liverpool (Birkenhead) England
Larne Northern Ireland	⇄	Cairnryan Scotland
Belfast Northern Ireland	⇄	Douglas Isle of Man
Belfast Northern Ireland	⇄	Holyhead Wales

Note: The Isle of Man is an island between Great Britain and Ireland. It is not part of the United Kingdom.

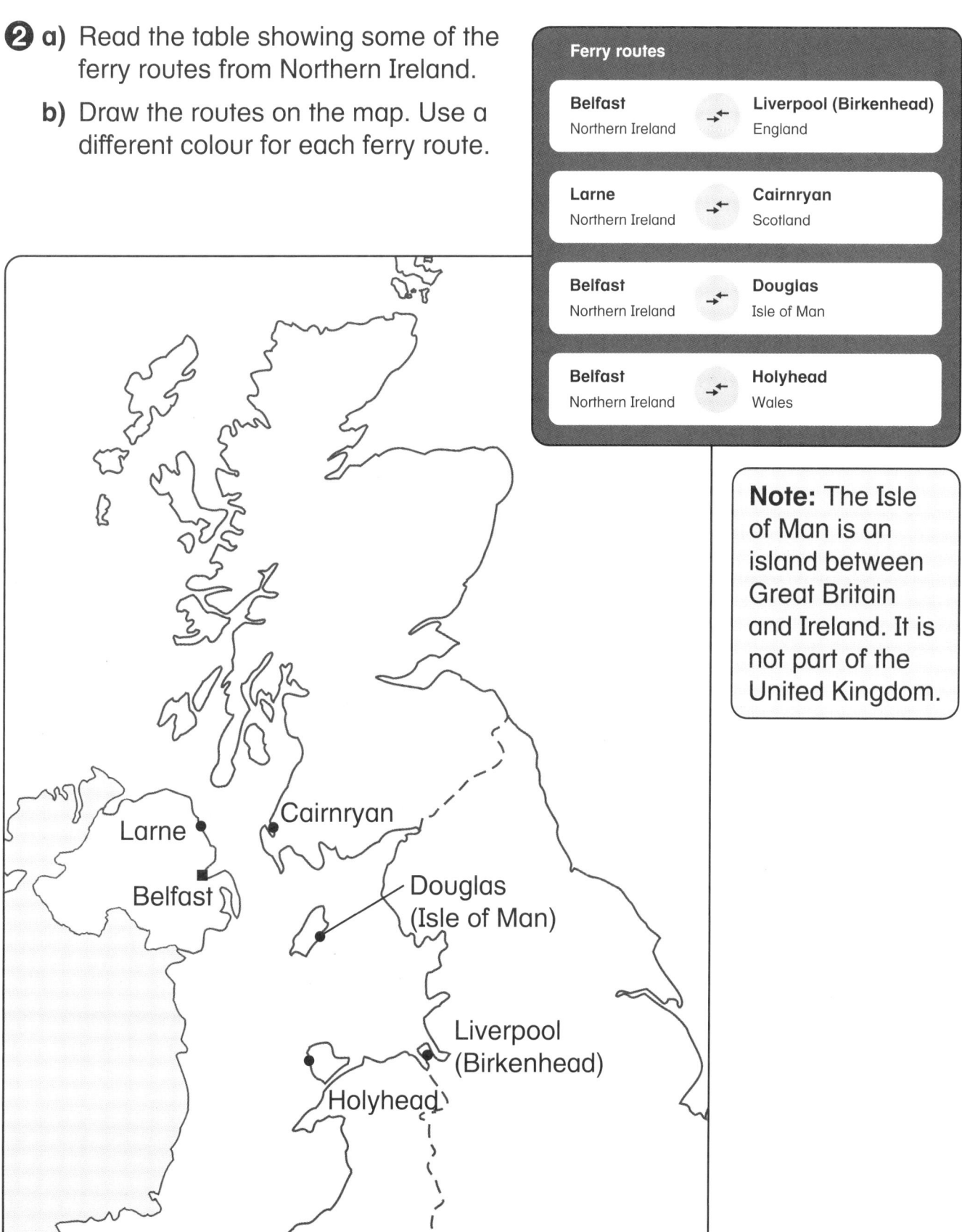

→ Supports Pupil Book Mapwork, page 39

Unit 7 — Northern Ireland

Lesson 2: Living in Northern Ireland

1 a) Make a comic strip to show a day in the life of Sienna and Patrick O'Neill. Draw pictures in each of the boxes to match the text.

①
The bus arrives at 8:00 a.m. to take Sienna and Patrick to school.

②
The bus travels through the countryside and to the town of Maghera, where their school is.

③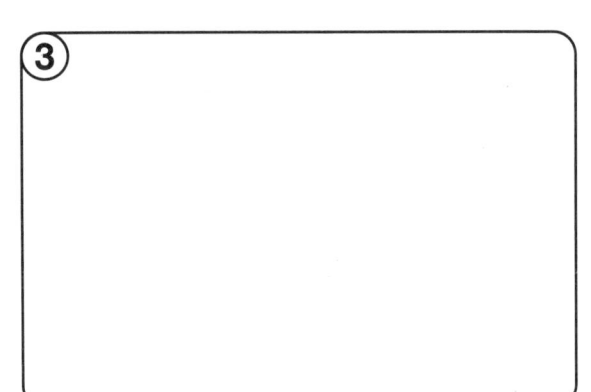
After school, Sienna and Patrick help their parents collect the cows for milking.

④
It starts to rain when Sienna and Patrick go inside for their dinner.

b) How is your life the same or different to Sienna and Patrick's? Write your ideas.

_____

_____

_____

Unit 7 Northern Ireland

2 What makes peat bogs like Ballynahone Bog special? Make a plan for a presentation to answer this question. Research the answers to the questions.

Introduction   What is a peat bog? <u>Peat bogs are very wet areas of land that contain a lot of peat. Peat bogs are special habitats for many plants and animals. They also protect the environment by safely storing harmful carbon.</u>   What is peat made of? <u>Peat is a type of soil that is made from dead plants that haven't rotted away.</u>
Section 1: Peat bogs in Northern Ireland   Where can you find peat bogs in Northern Ireland?   _____
Section 2: Plants and creatures, and peat bogs   What are two animals and two plants that live on peat bogs? Write a fact about each one.   Animal 1: _____   Animal 2: _____   Plant 1: _____   Plant 2: _____
Section 3: People and peat bogs   What do people use peat for?   _____   _____
Conclusion   Why is it important to look after peat bogs?   _____   _____

→ Supports Pupil Book Climate change, page 41

Unit 7 Northern Ireland

Lesson 3: A journey to Londonderry (Derry)

❶ Read page 42 of your Pupil Book, about the journey the O'Neill family take from Ballyknock Farm to go shopping in Londonderry (Derry).

a) Draw a simple symbol for each feature they pass on their journey.

Glenshane Pass	Dungiven Castle	Farm	Ness Wood

Hint: Glenshane Pass is a road that cuts through mountains.

b) Draw your symbols on the correct places on the map.

c) Starting at Ballyknock Farm, colour in the route the O'Neills take when they drive to Londonderry (Derry).

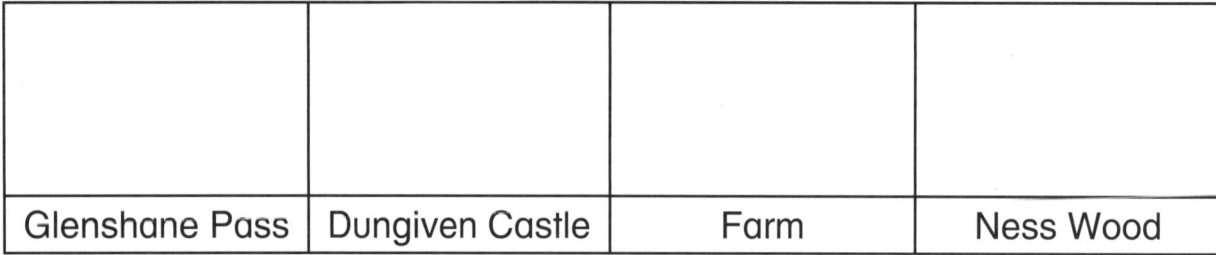

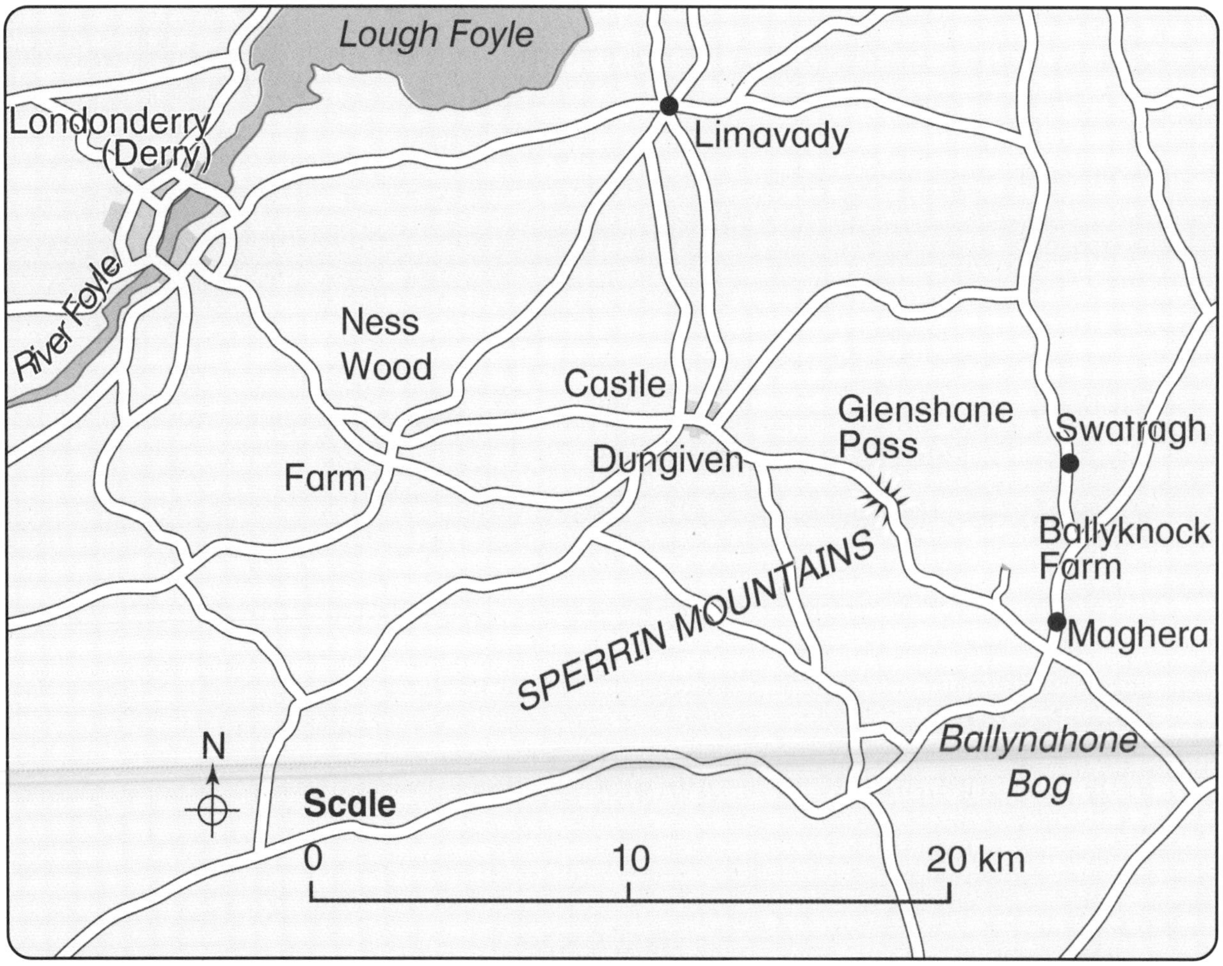

→ Supports Pupil Book Mapwork, page 43

Unit 7 Northern Ireland

2 a) Use this plan to design a brochure for tourists, to encourage them to visit Londonderry (Derry). Make notes in each section of the plan.

Brochure title: _____
Introduction: What information would be useful for tourists? For example, where is Londonderry (Derry)? What are some interesting facts about the city?   _____   _____   _____
Top spots: Describe four places that tourists might like to visit.

b) Now make your brochure on a separate sheet of paper.

- Fold the paper into four sections.
- Use the inside four sections to show the top spots to visit. Add pictures.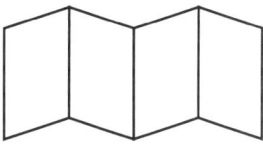
- Add the title and introduction to the front. Use big, bold letters and add a picture.
- You can add more of your own ideas to the back.

→ Supports Pupil Book Investigation, page 43

Unit 8 Germany

Lesson 1: Introducing Germany

1 Look at this map of Germany. Add labels to show the names and locations of:

a) the capital city

b) two more big cities

c) the biggest river

d) the biggest mountain.

Hint: Look at Pupil Book page 45.

2 Nine countries share a border with Germany. Can you name them all?

_____   _____   _____

_____   _____   _____

_____   _____   _____

Unit 8 Germany

❸ Use the information on pages 44 and 45 of your Pupil Book to think of five interesting questions about Germany.

a) Write your questions here, and leave space for the answers.

Question 1: _____

Answer: _____

Question 2: _____

Answer: _____

Question 3: _____

Answer: _____

Question 4: _____

Answer: _____

Question 5: _____

Answer: _____

b) Swap your book with a friend and answer each other's questions.

→ Supports Pupil Book Investigation, page 44

Unit 8 Germany

Lesson 2: The Ruhr: An industrial region

1 Find the towns and rivers of the Ruhr in the wordsearch puzzle.

Dinslaken   Duisburg   Essen   Dortmund
Bochum   Lippe   Rhine   Ruhr

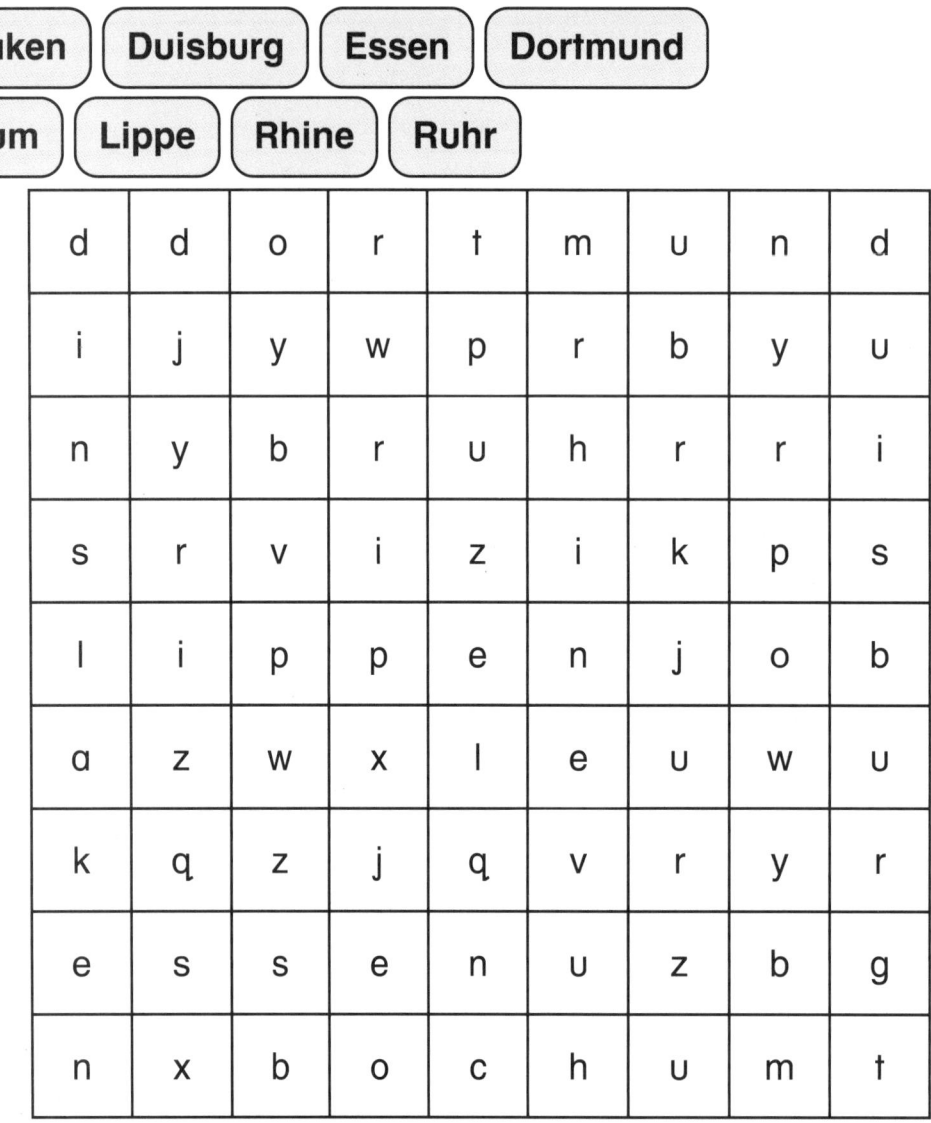

2 Use the words from the boxes to write five sentences about the Ruhr.

coal mine and iron works   new factories   new technology
railway   markets

_____

_____

_____

_____

Unit 8   Germany

❸ Look at these two photographs of different areas in Dinslaken.

Use the information on pages 48 and 49 of your Pupil Book to write a detailed caption for each photograph.

town

_____

_____

factories

_____

_____

47

Unit 8 Germany

Lesson 3: Living in Dinslaken

1 a) Draw pictures of four events in Dinslaken's history and add dates to make a simple timeline.

b) Write a sentence to describe each picture.

Hint: Order the events from the longest ago at the top to the most recent at the bottom.

→ Supports Pupil Book Investigation, page 49

Unit 8 Germany

❷ Imagine you have travelled to Dinslaken, to visit a family member.

Write an email to a friend at home. Describe the town and the places you have visited. How is it different or similar to where you live? Write at least two paragraphs.

From:

To:

Subject:

Unit 9 North America

Lesson 1: Introducing North America

1 What have you learnt about North America? Read the clues and complete the crossword puzzle.

Clues across

2 In Canada, there are great expanses of c_____ forest.

5 The M_____ civilisation built pyramids in the Mexican rainforest 3000 years ago.

6 Large spikey plants that grow in the Arizona Desert are called _____ plants.

Clues down

1 The R_____ M_____ stretch from Canada to Mexico.

3 Cities like New York have tall buildings, which are called s_____.

4 North America is bordered by the _____ Ocean to the west.

Unit 9 North America

② Use a dictionary to write a definition for each of these words.

a) rainforest	
b) grassland	
c) desert	
d) coniferous forest	

③ Look at pictures 1–5 on pages 50 and 51 of your Pupil Book. Which place would you most like to visit? Write a paragraph explaining:

- where the place is
- why you would like to visit it.

_____

_____

_____

_____

④ Research another place in the United States that you would like to visit.

a) Draw a picture of it.

b) Find a photograph of the same place for a class display.

→ Supports Pupil Book Investigation, page 51

Unit 9 North America

Lesson 2: Finding out about Canada

1 Look at the map of Canada on page 53 of your Pupil Book. Write the names of the provinces and territories in the spaces.

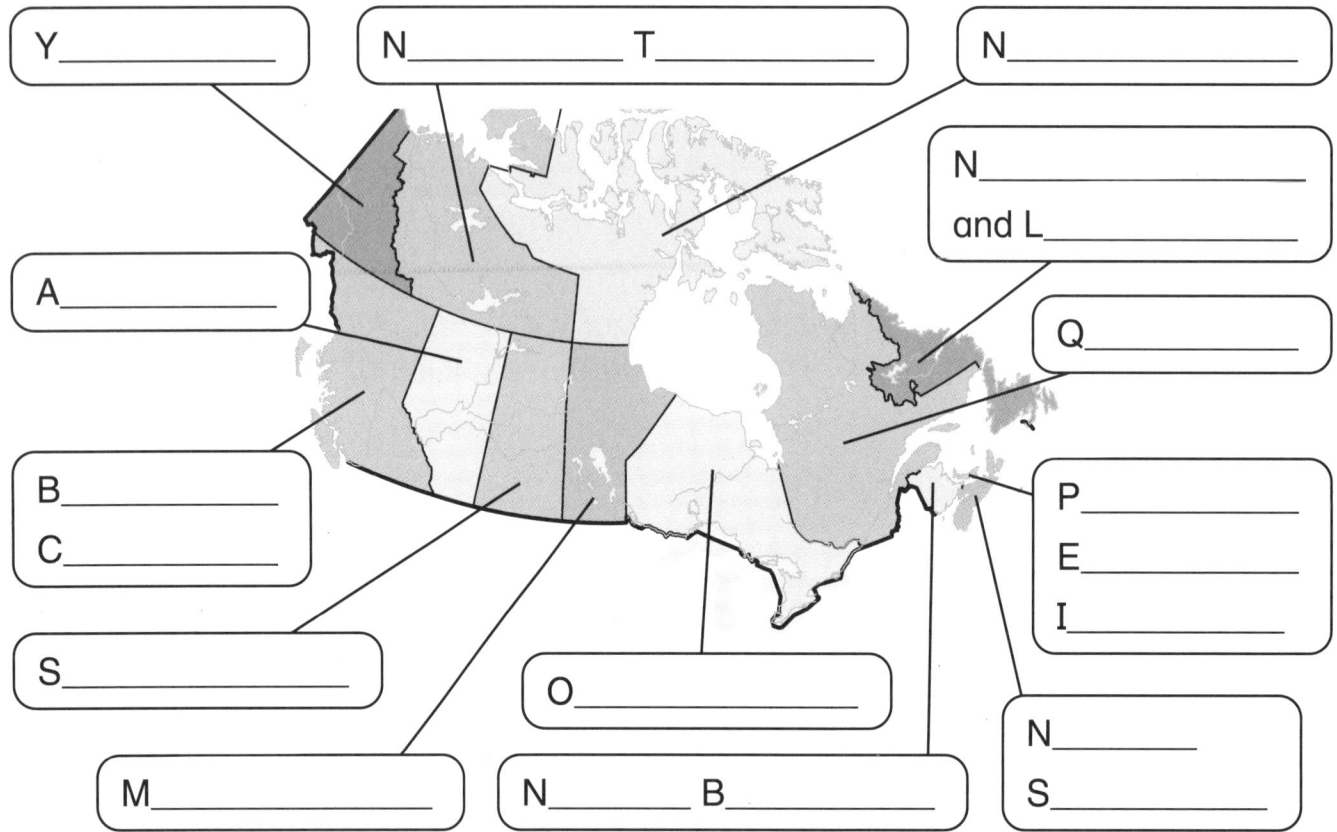

- Y_____
- N_____ T_____
- N_____
- N_____ and L_____
- A_____
- Q_____
- B_____
- C_____
- P_____ E_____ I_____
- S_____
- O_____
- N_____ S_____
- M_____
- N_____ B_____

Note: See how the boundary lines between the provinces and territories are often straight. This is because they often follow lines of latitude and longitude.

These are imaginary lines that help us to locate where a place is in the world.

- **Lines of latitude** show how far north or south from the equator somewhere is.

- **Lines of longitude** run from the top to the bottom of the Earth. They show how far east or west a place is from the equator.

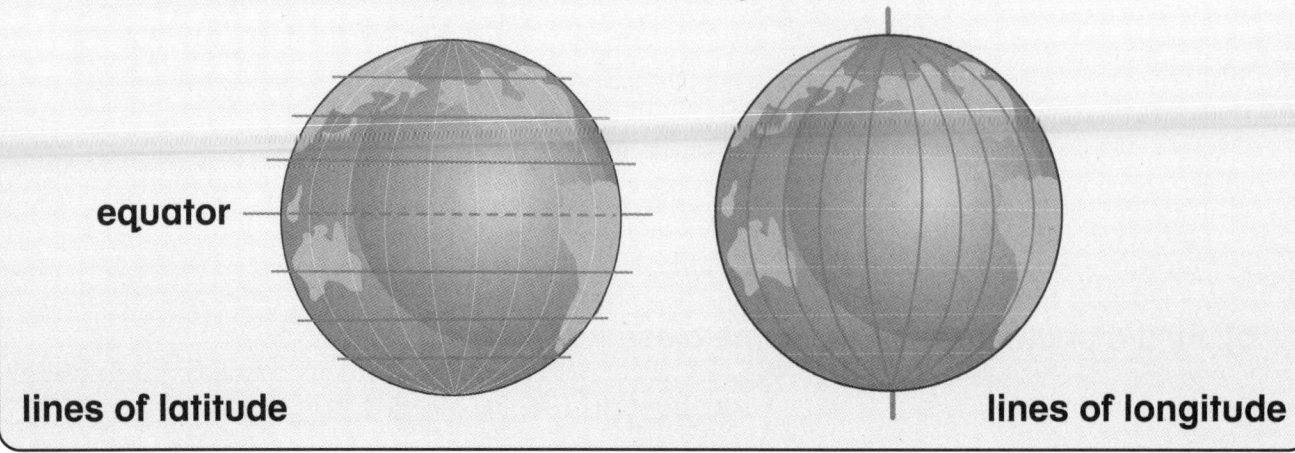

lines of latitude   lines of longitude

52

Unit 9   North America

❷ Use the information on pages 52 and 53 of your Pupil Book to write five interesting questions about Canada.

a) Write your questions here, and leave space for the answers.

Question 1: _____
_____
Answer: _____
_____

Question 2: _____
_____
Answer: _____
_____

Question 3: _____
_____
Answer: _____
_____

Question 4: _____
_____
Answer: _____
_____

Question 5: _____
_____
Answer: _____
_____

b) Swap your book with a friend and answer each other's questions.

Unit 9 North America

Lesson 3: Crossing the Rockies

❶ Mark the route of the Trans-Canadian Highway on the map below.
- Use the map on page 54 of your Pupil Book as a guide.
- Start in Calgary and end in Vancouver.
- Mark each place the route passes through.

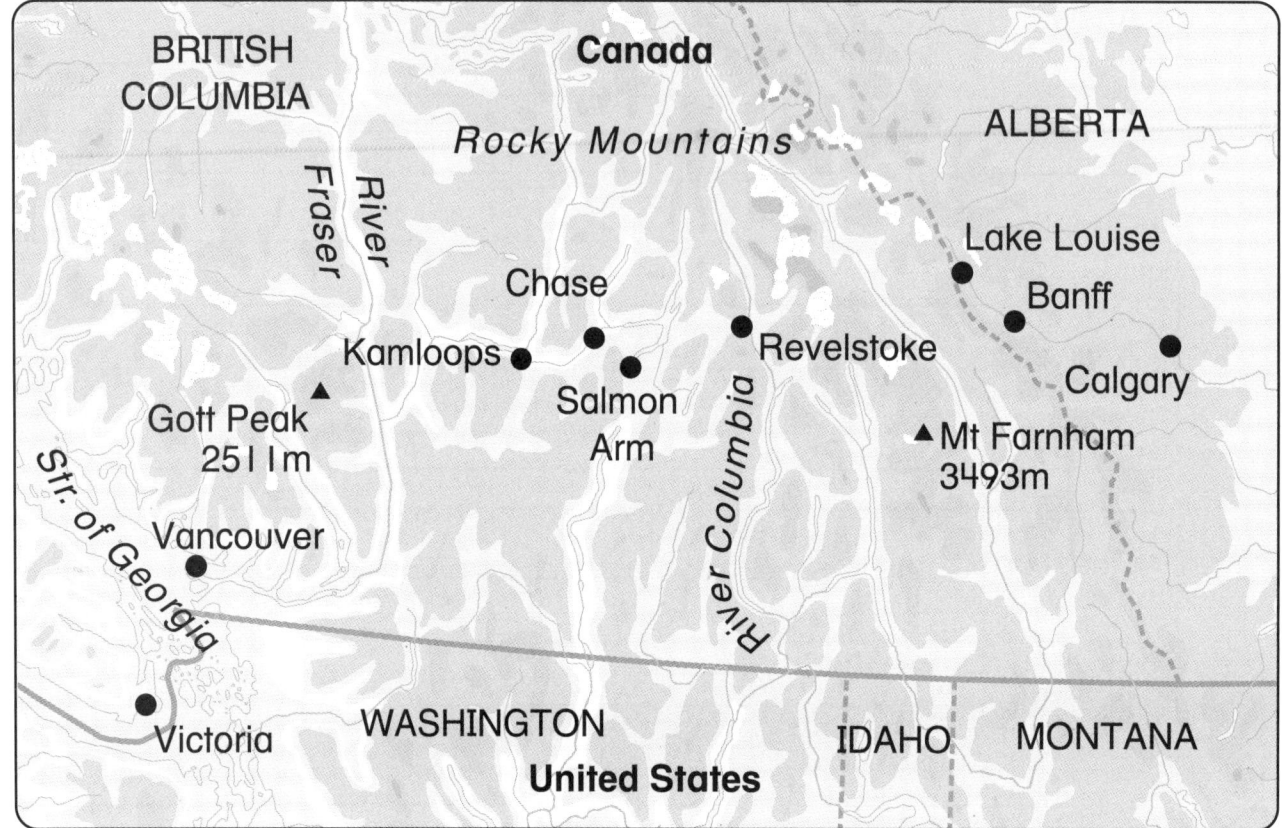

❷ Make a list of wild animals that live in the Rocky Mountains.

→ Supports Pupil Book Mapwork, page 55

_____   _____

_____   _____

_____   _____

_____   _____

_____   _____

Hint: Two animals are named in your Pupil Book. Can you research any more?

Unit 9   North America

❸ Look at the four photographs below. How do they link with the Trans-Canada Highway and the Rocky Mountains? Write a sentence to describe each photograph.

Parts of the Trans-Canada Highway pass through flat landscape.

❹ Make a slideshow presentation with six slides about the Trans-Canada Highway and the Rocky Mountains. You can use photographs like the ones above.

→ Supports Pupil Book Investigation, page 55

Unit 10   Asia

Lesson 1: The Gulf

1 Look at the photographs. What do they tell us about life in the Gulf? Write a caption for each. Can you use all the words from the boxes?

| oil reserves | species | dates | fish | climate | desert |

a)

b)

c)

Unit 10   Asia

2 Find out what items in and around your classroom or home are made of oil. Make a list.

Hint: Did you know that many plastic items are made of oil?

_____   _____

_____   _____

_____   _____

_____   _____

→ Supports Pupil Book Investigation, page 57

3 a) Draw two items made of plastic that you think you cannot live without.

b) Could these items be made out of a different material to plastic? Write your ideas below.

_____

_____

_____

Unit 10 Asia

Lesson 2: Learning about the United Arab Emirates

1 Look at the picture of the Burj Khalifa. It is about 830 meters in height!

a) Find out what the tallest building in your country or continent is. How tall is it?

Name of building: _____ Height: _____ metres

b) Draw a cross to show the height of your tallest building on the meter scale. Use a ruler to draw a horizontal line across the page at this height.

c) Draw a picture of your building in the space next to the Burj Khalifa. Ensure the top touches your line you drew in Activity b).

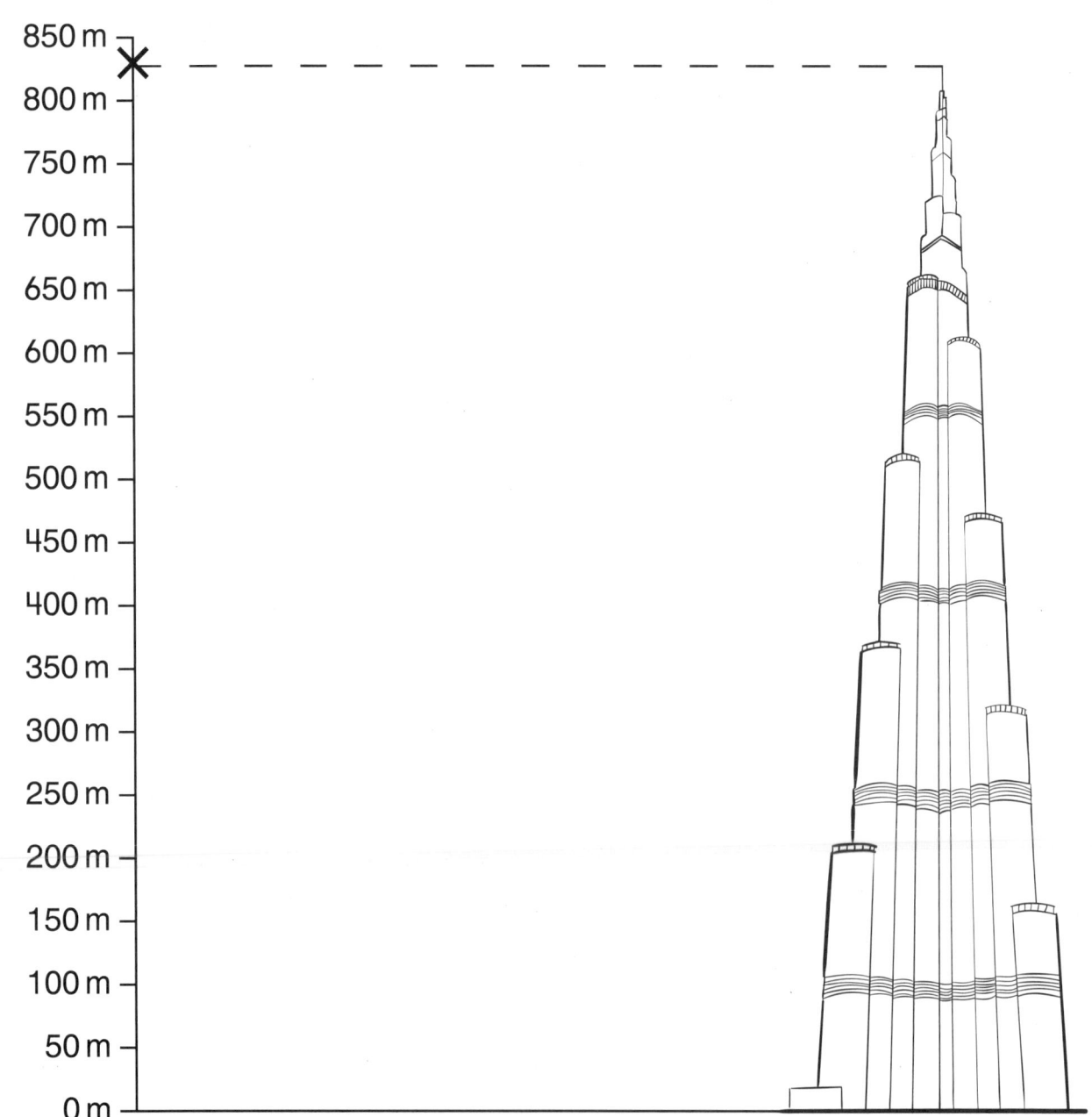

Unit 10   Asia

2 Colour the flag of the United Arab Emirates.

3 a) Research and write a few sentences about how the Palm Islands at Dubai were created.

_____

_____

_____

b) Draw a picture of different palm islands in the United Arab Emirates.

c) Find some photographs of the different palm islands for a class display.

➜ Supports Pupil Book Investigation, page 59

Unit 10 Asia

Lesson 3: Exploring the United Arab Emirates

1 Look at the pie chart on page 60 of your Pupil Book.

   a) What are the names of six countries in Asia that buy oil from the UAE?

_____ _____ _____

_____ _____ _____

   b) On the map, draw the routes that oil might take to get to these countries. Use a different colour for each route.

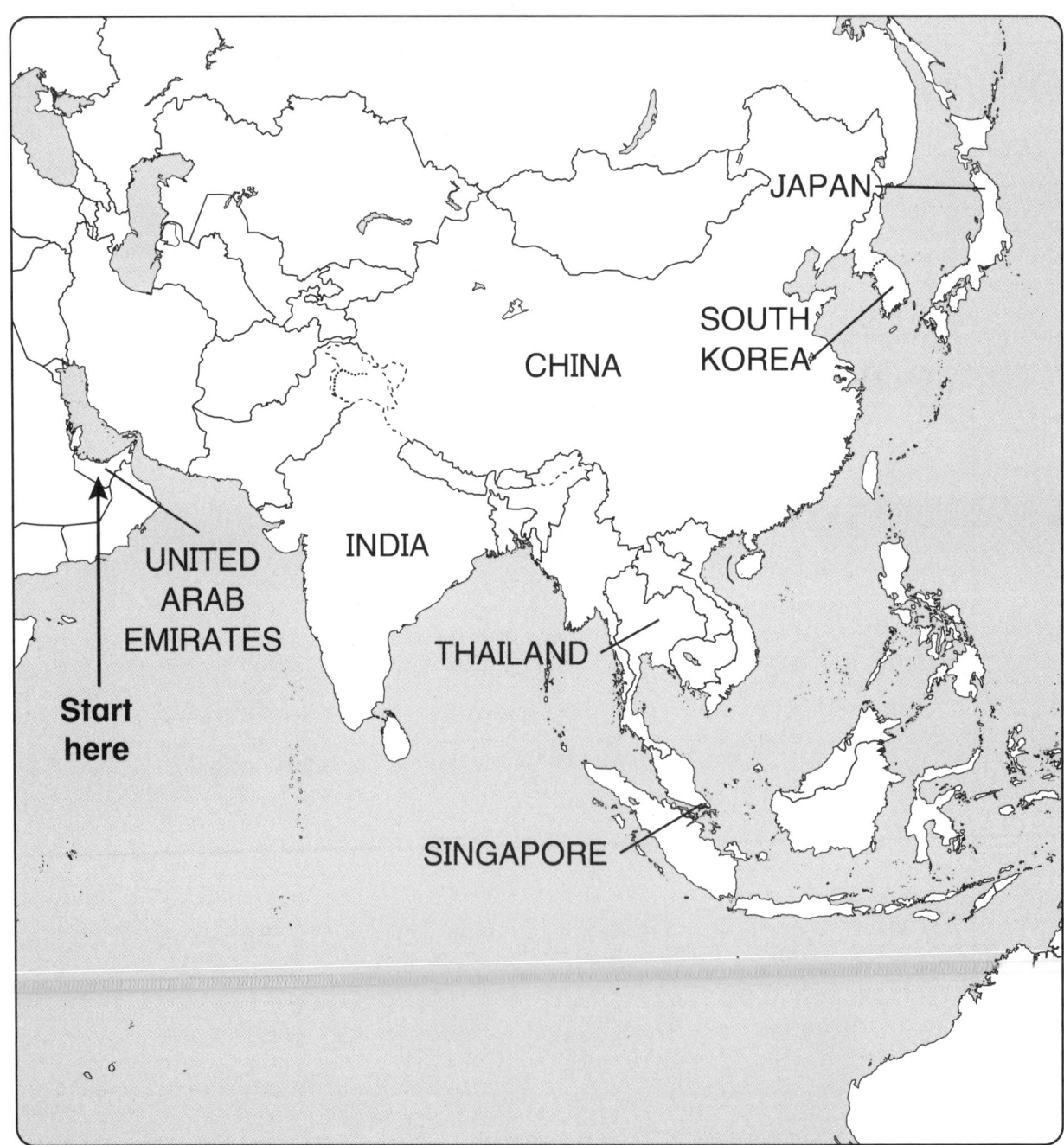

→ Supports Pupil Book Mapwork, page 61

Unit 10   Asia

2 a) Complete this fact file about the geographical features of the UAE.

Fact file	
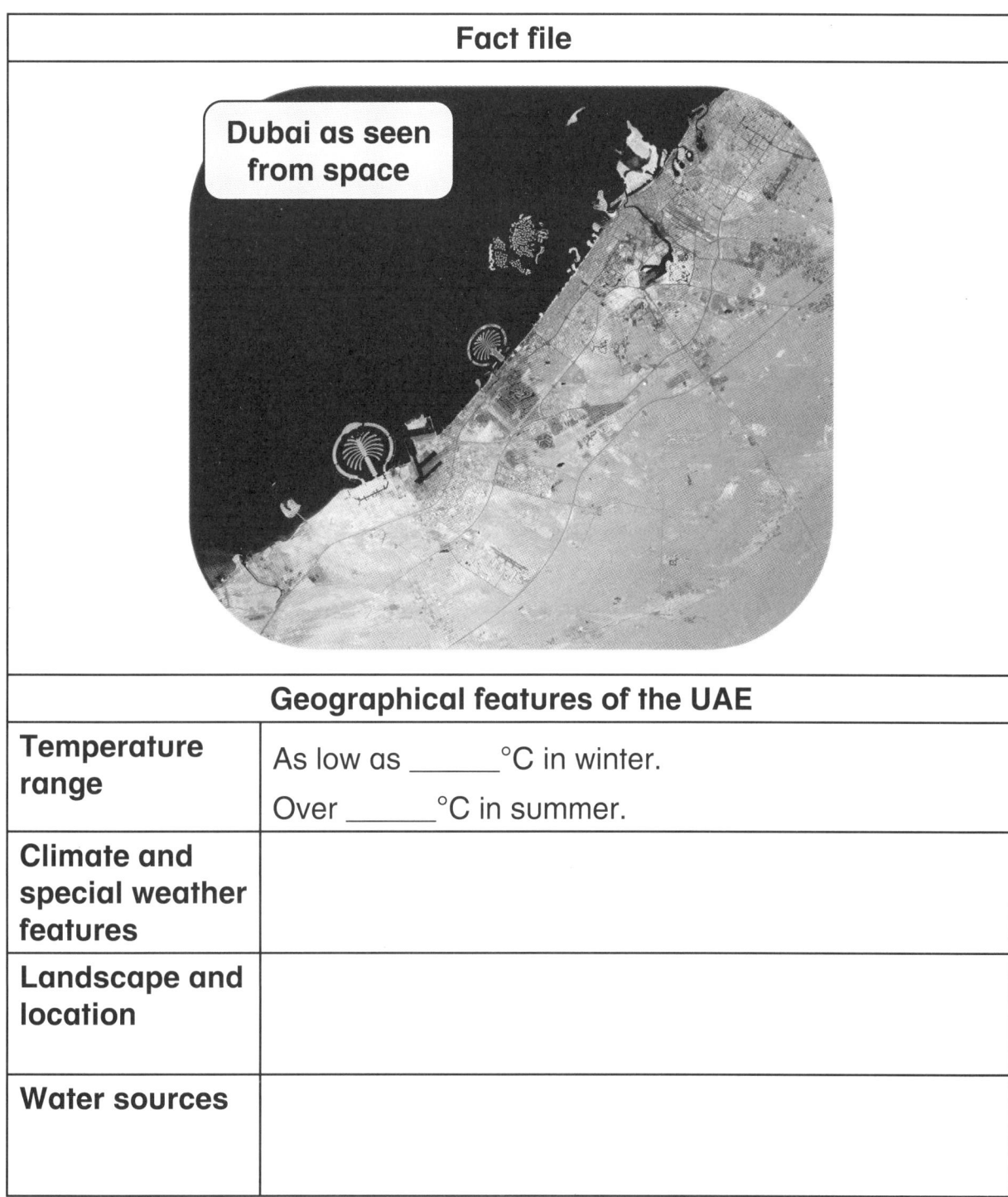 Dubai as seen from space	
Geographical features of the UAE	
Temperature range	As low as _____ °C in winter. Over _____ °C in summer.
Climate and special weather features	
Landscape and location	
Water sources	

b) How do the people in the UAE adapt to live in this environment?
Think about:

- clothing _____
- drinking water _____
- keeping cool _____
- buildings _____

Notes

William Collins' dream of knowledge for all began with the publication of his first book in 1819.

A self-educated mill worker, he not only enriched millions of lives, but also founded a flourishing publishing house. Today, staying true to this spirit, Collins books are packed with inspiration, innovation and practical expertise.
They place you at the centre of a world of possibility and give you exactly what you need to explore it.

Published by Collins
An imprint of HarperCollins*Publishers*
The News Building, 1 London Bridge Street, London, SE1 9GF, UK

HarperCollins*Publishers*
Macken House, 39/40 Mayor Street Upper, Dublin 1, D01 C9W8, Ireland

Browse the complete Collins catalogue at
collins.co.uk

© HarperCollins*Publishers* Limited 2025
Maps © Collins Bartholomew 2025

10 9 8 7 6 5 4 3 2 1

ISBN 978-0-00-872837-3

All rights reserved. No part of this publication may be reproduced, stored in a retrieval system, or transmitted in any form by any means, electronic, mechanical, photocopying, recording or otherwise, without the prior written permission of the Publisher or a licence permitting restricted copying in the United Kingdom issued by the Copyright Licensing Agency Ltd, 5th Floor, Shackleton House, 4 Battle Bridge Lane, London SE1 2HX.

Without limiting the author's and publisher's exclusive rights, any unauthorised use of this publication to train generative artificial intelligence (AI) technologies is expressly prohibited. HarperCollins also exercise their rights under Article 4(3) of the Digital Single Market Directive 2019/790 and expressly reserve this publication from the text and data mining exception.

British Library Cataloguing-in-Publication Data

A catalogue record for this publication is available from the British Library.

Author: Fiona Macgregor
Publisher: Laura White
Product managers: Natasha Paul and Shelley Teasdale
Development editor: Judith Walters
Copyeditor: Charlotte Christensen
Proofreader: Charlotte Christensen
Cover designer and illustrator: Steve Evans
Internal illustrator: Jouve India Private Ltd
Typesetter: David Jimenez
Production controller: Katie Jean-Baptiste
Printed and bound in the UK by Martins the Printers

This book is produced from independently certified FSC™ paper to ensure responsible forest management.

For more information visit: www.harpercollins.co.uk/green
collins.co.uk/sustainability

Acknowledgements

The publishers gratefully acknowledge the permission granted to reproduce the copyright material in this book. Every effort has been made to trace copyright holders and to obtain their permission for the use of copyright material. The publishers will gladly receive any information enabling them to rectify any error or omission at the first opportunity.

All photos: Shutterstock.